The 7 Secrets of Happiness
How to Bring Joy into Your Everyday Life

By

Linda Johnson & Kat McDivitt

AB **ANGELICO BOOKS**

OTHER BOOKS BY LINDA JOHNSON

Intuition – Your Most Powerful Tool

How To Talk To Your Kids & Grandkids: 10 Secrets To Being the Grandmother Everyone Adores

Giving from the Heart: 57 Ways to Show Your Love (also called Giving from the Love Languages: 57 Ways To Show Your Love)

Beginning Meditation for Busy People: How To Get More Done, Feel Less Stressed, & Be Happier

The Seven Secrets of Happiness: How To Bring Joy Into Your Everyday Life

OTHER BOOKS BY MARIA JOHNSON

The Power of Sleep: How to Get to Sleep and Stay Asleep Naturally

Pain Relief: The Drug Free Way To Feel Better Fast

How To Eliminate Your Allergies Forever: The Truth About Allergic Reactions, Allergy Symptoms and Allergy Relief

To learn more about these books and buy copies, please visit: www.AngelicoBooks.com

TABLE OF CONTENTS

Introduction

It is a great pleasure to write this introduction. I have known one of the authors, Kat McDivitt for many years, and have seen the results she has achieved by applying the techniques discussed in this little book. Several of them I have used in my own life and have recommended to clients when I was working as a psychotherapist. Here you will find seven ways to change your life for the better.

This book is short and concise and can be easily read in a couple of hours. Of course, it is only by actually practicing these techniques on a daily basis that their benefits will really become apparent.

However I am convinced that if you do that, and keep doing so, you will obtain much more than what you may now call "happiness."

– Kenneth C. Turner
PhD (Physics, Princeton, 1962)
MA (Humanistic and Transpersonal Psychology,
University of West Georgia, 2007)

Happiness:
How to Get It and Keep It!

Introduction

Are you willing to be happier than you've ever felt before? Are you interested in learning how to wake up happy every day and feel happy consistently?

What if I told you there were some simple shifts that you can make in your life today that will help you be happier for the rest of your life?

Would you be willing to give me 2 hours of your life to try it out? That's about the time it takes to watch a bad movie, but in that same time you could change the movie of your life for the better.

Interested?

Here's what it's all about.

One of the basic life recipes we've been given is wrong. We're taught that if we work hard, earn more, buy more, be more successful, then we'll be happy.

While this may seem trite, and obviously untrue both metaphorically and realistically, this is the life that most people actually strive toward.

And, for the most part, they are not happy.

We are trained almost from birth that happiness is just around the corner. The next great job, the promotion, the car, losing the weight, getting the new partner.

Recent research is showing us what we've known at a gut level for a long time. Happiness is not about having more, doing more, and getting more. It really comes from an internal shift.

We need to let go of the story that happiness is something we can buy, that we can get happier through changes in our external world, and start to make small, simple shifts in our internal world.

Being happy is actually easier than what we've been taught.

How do we (Linda and Kat) know this?

Well, we've been around the block a bit. Linda has been a counselor for 30 years, and worked with all sorts of people, she comes from a classical therapy background. Kat comes from a more radical background, and we'll start with her story.

Kat's story:

I spent a lot of time in my life being depressed. In my early childhood I was happy, rich and carefree. When I was three, I was in a plane crash, lost my sister, and ended up in a broken family in poverty. What I learned from that is that money leads to stability and happiness. So I focused for years on earning more money.

All in all I did pretty well. I built businesses and sold them. I traveled the world. I eventually had everything I thought I wanted. Except happiness.

I remember a moment, sitting on a yacht off Honolulu harbor watching the fireworks and feeling miserable.

Later that night I ran into a Tibetan nun who was happy with almost nothing. She just exuded happiness. In our conversation she showed me very clearly the ways that I had been trained to look at happiness all wrong.

It started me on a ten year journey that took me from Honolulu to the mountains of Colorado, the rice fields of Bali and the learning centers of Rome, London and Paris.

I studied the latest thinking on Happiness – the actual science of what makes people happy. I tried and tested. I learned from yogis and scientists.

Once I felt like I had a system, I tried it out on people – friends, clients, myself, honing and distilling until I felt like I had the absolute nuggets. The things that could make the biggest difference in shortest amount of time with the least effort.

I shared my ideas with my friend and mentor Linda, and we decided to merge our experience to help people attain higher levels of happiness than they have ever felt before, a consistent happiness from the time they wake up, to the time they go to sleep.

7 Myths About Happiness

MYTH: I'll be happy when I'm in the right relationship or get my dream job.

TRUTH: Happiness is the side effect of a process, not the result of attaining some goal.

MYTH: The best years of my life are over.
TRUTH: There's a new research study out of the UK that looked at 300,000 people and determined that people are actually most satisfied with their lives between the ages of 65 and 79. (http://www.ons.gov.uk/peoplepopulationandcommunity/wellbeing/articles/measuringnationalwellbeing/atwhatageispersonalwellbeingthehighest)

MYTH: It's selfish to focus on your happiness. This is a dangerous myth. One client I worked with last week felt like she could never be happy when there is suffering in the world. Another one is happy people are self-centered. Finally, many people, especially women often feel like they must put the happiness of their family above their own. They feel extremely guilty if they are happy and others in their family are not.
TRUTH: Studies show that happier people tend to be more helpful, do more volunteer work and contribute more. So the best way to make more of a contribution to others is to be happy yourself.

MYTH: I can make him/her happy. Many times people feel that they can "make" someone happy. I've tried this myself with friends and loved ones who were not happy. I would cook for them and care for them as best as I could in order to "make" them happy. It never worked.
TRUTH: For someone to be happy, they need to make a

choice, either consciously or unconsciously that they are willing to be happy. Once they decide on happiness, they are going to be much better at managing their own happiness than you could ever be. However tempting it is to try to control someone else's happiness, it rarely works.

MYTH: If someone just did "X" then I would be happy. Often I hear this in couples. If he just communicated better. If she just wanted to have more sex. Then I'd be happy. **TRUTH:** Of course there are things that others can do that might help us to create the feeling of happiness inside of us. This is part of what makes us work as a society and culture. On the other hand, our ability to actually experience that happiness, or choose to experience that event as happy, is our own.

Definition of happiness

So what is happiness? According to the online Merriam Webster Dictionary, happiness is either of two things: a state of well-being and contentment or a pleasurable or satisfying experience. These definitions are a little bit of a simplification so let us see how the wise people of history say about happiness.

Alice Walker – "Don't wait around for other people to be happy for you. Any happiness you get you've got to make yourself."

Plato – "The human soul consists of three parts: The reason, the will and the desire. A man is happy when all three parts of the soul are in balance."

Aristotle – "Happiness is the meaning and the purpose of life, the whole aim and end of human existence."

Martha Washington – "I am determined to be cheerful and happy in whatever situation I may find myself. For I have learned that the greater part of our misery or unhappiness is determined not by our circumstance but by our disposition."

Buddha – "Happiness comes when your work and words are of benefit to yourself and others."

Erich Fromm –Described true happiness as deriving, not from momentary pleasure, but from human growth.

Abraham Lincoln –"People are just as happy as they make up their minds to be."

Maya Angelou – "If you don't like something, change it. If you can't change it, change your attitude."

Dalai Lama – "Happiness is not something readymade. It comes from your own actions."

Franklin Roosevelt – "Happiness lies in the joy of achievement and the thrill of creative effort."

Mahatma Gandhi – "Happiness is when what you think, what you say, and what you do are in harmony."

Sandra Bullock – "I think most of us are raised with preconceived notions of the choices we're supposed to make. We waste so much time making decisions based on someone else's idea of our happiness – what will make you a good citizen or a good wife or daughter or actress. Nobody says, 'Just be happy – go be a cobbler or go live with goats.'"

William Shakespeare –"Sweet are the uses of adversity which, like the toad, ugly and venomous, wears yet a precious jewel in his head."

Most of the above definitions are related to our 7 secrets to happiness. If you study what these learned people have said, you'll realize that all of their definitions involve our participation and some action and decision-making on our part.

What do we mean by happiness is a practice?

Happiness is your personal responsibility. Never give the power to make you happy or unhappy to anyone or to anything else. We can share with you our secret to happiness, But in the final analysis, it will be you who will decide what you will do with these secrets.

Happiness is both a choice and a habit.

Many of us underestimate the amount of control that we have over our own happiness.

For a few lucky people, happiness comes easily and naturally. For most of us, we need to find out what makes us really happy and then practice until we perfect it. None of us was born knowing how to talk or drive a car. Driving a car or learning to talk will benefit us and perhaps add to our pleasure. So we practice until we're good enough to master the skills. The same is true with happiness. If you want to be happy or increase your happiness, you need to practice being happy every day of your life.

Here is a Cherokee story we've adapted for this book:

A young boy came to his grandfather feeling anger and sadness because a friend had done him an injustice. The grandfather said, "Let me tell you a story.

"I have felt anger, sadness, and fear when the people and systems around me seem to take so much and give so little.

"But these feelings wear you down and do not hurt your enemy. It's like taking a poison and wishing your enemy would die. I have struggled with these feelings many times.

"It's as if there are two wolves fighting inside me. One is good and does no harm. He lives in harmony. He is full of joy, presence, peace, love, kindness and hope. The other wolf is full of anger, sadness, fear, self-pity, guilt, – the smallest incident will send him into anger and despair.

"Sometimes it's hard to live with these two wolves inside of me, for both of them want to have control, and the world around me supports the angry wolf."

The boy looked seriously into his Grandfather's eyes and asked, "Which one wins, Grandfather?"

The grandfather smiled and said, "The one I feed".

Each of us has two wolves inside us that are fed by our habits, our choices and our thoughts. When we learn to feed the positive wolf more, it shows up in our lives as happiness and ease. This book is about giving you tools to feed the positive wolf.

The 7 secrets to happiness contain some simple disciplines or habits that you can practice every day to achieve h r people say or do to you is not all about you, but about *them*. When you practice optimism and self love and getting connected with your soul, you are also practicing happiness.

CHAPTER 1

Overview of the 7 Secrets to Happiness

Through life experience, many workshops, reading and studying and applying the research on happiness, I've created a formula that distills the basic concepts of all of this learning into 7 simple secrets.

Secret 1

The 1st secret is about living in the here and now or savoring the moment; letting go of the past and avoiding worrying about the future; understanding why it's important to live in the present and discovering the reasons why you find it difficult to do this. We will also show you how to savor the special moments and give you a step-by-step way of doing it.

Secret 2

Take control of your life. Life doesn't just happen; you have to make it happen. So many people seem to be just waiting for whatever life will bring them. What's holding you back from 'taking the bull by the horns and directing life where you want it to go? The reasons could be fear: fear of failure, rejection, making a wrong decision, and fear of confronting reality. Perhaps some beliefs restrict you from aggressively pursuing what you want from life, and lastly, you may be constantly listening to that inner voice or the inner critic that is telling you "You can't do it.", "You don't have what it takes to succeed", or "It's too difficult".

In this book we will show you how to take control of your life by confronting your fears and repudiating that inner critic inside of you. We will also show you how to actively control your life by changing your thoughts about yourself.

Secret 3

Another important secret to happiness is to "Act as If" or act as if everything that you want is already at your fingertips. This premise or concept is actually espoused by the advocates of the "Law of Attraction", – that any-thing you want bad enough, you attract. There is even a documentary movie of the same title "Act As If" that is truly inspiring. In this book we will explore this concept and explain its relation to happiness, and then, show you how to fake it till you make it.

Secret 4

The next secret to happiness is "Don't Take Anything Personally," meaning, what others do or say is not about You, but about the doer's projection of his own reality. We will explore the benefits of this concept and also show you the techniques for not taking things personally and how to practice these techniques.

Secret 5

Be an optimist. Focus on the positives rather than the negatives and learn why it is important for you to be an optimist. Here we will show you ways to be optimistic and practice optimism in your day-to-day activities.

Secret 6

Loving yourself or self love is another secret to happiness. Self love sounds trite, and it's one of the most important (and sometimes difficult) steps you can take that will dramatically increase your happiness. Taking care of your mind and body are ways of loving yourself so in this chapter we will discuss how to do this.

Secret 7

Connect with your soul. Your soul is where you will find who you really are. Connecting with your soul will help you to find happiness and your passion. We will help you find ways to connect with your soul, learning to quiet yourself through meditation, how to feed your soul and how to connect with others.

Lastly, we will show you how positive thinking connects you to your soul.

The decision to be happy or not is yours to make. We include practical, realistic and doable exercises that will help you use these secrets, and with discipline, you will achieve the happiness that you're looking for.

The 7 Secrets to Happiness

To recap, let me give you the 7 secrets to happiness:

- Savor the Moment (be in the present)
- Take Control of Your Life
- Act As If/Fake it till you make it
- Don't take anything personally
- Practice Optimism
- Love yourself
- Connect with your soul

CHAPTER 2

1st Secret to Happiness – Savor the Moment (Be in the present)

"It is difficult to live in the present, ridiculous to live in the future, and impossible to live in the past. Nothing is as far away as one minute ago." – Jim Bishop

Do you spend your days regretful of the past and worrying about the future? This is a sure way to be miserable. You can never change the past and the future is unpredictable. In fact, according to one song "Tomorrow may never come". The only thing that you can control is the here and now; the only moment that you truly live is the present. You can only really take action in the present and you can only feel your feelings now – all decisions and actions are done in the present and all emotions are felt in the here and now.

Life happens in the present, and many people often ignore what's happening right now because they're preoccupied with the past and worrying about the future. How often do you find yourself on autopilot as your drive your car to work already thinking ahead to the work that awaits you at the office or looking back at the sales presentation you made yesterday and wondering whether it made any impact on your audience? Do you ever take time to savor your first cup of coffee or is your mind already rushing to the next task at hand?

Why Savor the Moment

Yes, there are times when you need to think of the past, the present and the future. With practice, you can learn to concentrate on the present more and really enjoy the moment.

I remember talking to a nun several years ago about this. My concern was that if I put all my efforts into living in the present, I would never get anything done. She assured me that even if I put my focus on living in the present every moment of the day, my mind was already so conditioned to slip into the past and future, that I would still be effective. I'd just enjoy it more. I have found her words to be true.

Why dwell on the past when you can't do anything about it? You can't change the past and fretting about the mistakes of the past will only make you miserable. The best value of thinking about the past is to evaluate what happened, learn from it and move on.

Benjamin Franklin, one of our country's forefathers, did this extremely well. At the end of every day he would review his day, consider the things that he would like to do differently, imagine doing them differently, and then let them go. The next morning he would start fresh and in the moment.

You also can not control the future. You can plan it and take some action in the present, such as making sound financial investments now. There are many uncontrollable factors that can affect your future – banks and insurance companies can go bankrupt, the economy could suffer and prices of stocks can drop or you can die tomorrow and never really enjoy the future. There are so many variables that affect the future. That does not mean that you should not plan for it. What is wrong is depriving yourself of enjoying the present because you're preparing for the future.

Change is inevitable. If you look at your life over the last 5 years, how much has changed? If you imagine yourself from 5 years ago, would that man or woman even conceive of the changes that have happened in your life? Consider the things that you might be worrying about right now: relationships, money, family. They seem very important, right? But, in one year, do you think these decisions and situations will feel as urgent in retrospect as they feel now?

You miss so much out of life when you dwell in the past or over-plan the future. Working hard to prepare for the future of your children because you don't want them to go through the hardships you suffered in your childhood, will not mean anything if you're not around while they are growing up or you're too overworked to be a part of their childhood. Enjoy your children now. They'll probably be happier, and so will you!

Here's a Buddhist story about living in the past and the present.

'Two monks were on a pilgrimage. One day they came to a deep fast river. At the edge of the river was a beautiful woman who was looking across the river.

The woman asked the monks if they would help her. The first monk turned his back. The members of their order were forbidden to touch women.

The second monk picked her up and carried her across the river. He put her down and continued on the pilgrimage.

The monks resumed their pilgrimage, the second monk in perfect harmony and enjoying the countryside. The first monk became more and more brooding and distracted. Finally he burst out, "Brother, we are taught to avoid contact with women, and you not only touched a woman, but you carried her on your shoulders!"

The second monk smiled at the first monk and said, "I only carried her across the river. You have been carrying her all day.'

Like the second monk, many of us tend to still be weighed down by thoughts of the past or future rather than enjoying the moment.

Advantages of living in the present

Being focused on the present has a lot of advantages or benefits, and these include:

- More intense enjoyment of life – When you savor the moment, the air you breathe is sweeter, the food you eat is tastier, you wake up with a smile, you have more fun with your family and even work can become more pleasant.

- More clarity of mind – When you are in the present you're more focused and thoughts and ideas flow smoothly and naturally to you. You perform well at school, at work and even at play.

- Less stress – Most of the time, dwelling on the past and worrying about the future can be very stressful. When you are savoring the moment, you are experiencing life, not worrying about it.

- More productivity – When you are savoring the moment you are calmer and more relaxed and centered or focused on what you're doing at the moment. This makes you more productive. You get things done. Concentrating on the task at hand rather than multi-tasking or thinking of many other things while doing one thing is a sure-fire formula for being more productive.

- Improved relationships – When you're really committed to whatever you're doing or of being at the moment with someone, then your relationships with your partner, your children and other members of the family, your friends, and your co-workers will be better.

- More positive – When you are savoring the moment there is no fear of the future or worry about the past so you are more positive about life.

When you savor the moment, being really present for whatever is happening, you feel more secure, more enthusiastic, more ardent and happier. You will notice a stronger sense of self, feel more self-confident and be more accepting of your own failings and limitations. Being aware of the here and now lessens the likelihood of suffering from attention problems, binge eating and/or depression. You can also accept criticism without feeling exposed and threatened. You are less aggressive and fight less with your peers, your lovers, and your superiors – improving your relationships with everybody in your orbit.

Let me give you an example. In my twenties I used to get extremely strong stomach cramps. They were so painful that they would make me sick. I would lie on the floor of the bathroom writhing in pain. After awhile I learned that even though the pain was intense, if I we present with it - if I stayed completely in the moment, breathing with the pain, it became more bearable. Being in the moment with the excruciating pain actually made me feel both more in control, and made the experience more bearable. It certainly didn't make me feel happy, but I was happier when I focus on being present with it that I was when I let myself descend into misery.

How to Savor the Moment

The masters of this art of living in the present are babies. When they feel pain or are hungry they cry. When they're happy they smile or laugh, not later – at the very moment that they feel the pain or are happy. You can't go back to being babies. You can re-learn to live in the present.

Although it might be hard to release the nagging thoughts that race through your minds, whether it's about the past or the future, there are techniques you can learn to do to help you seize the moment. Learning to live in the present or in the now is a skill, so give yourself time and really exert effort to learn the skill.

Focus on every action. Being consciously aware of everything that you do is one way to live in the now or the present. When you eat, focus on the act of eating, savor every morsel of food that you put into your mouth rather than thinking ahead of what you plan to do after eating. Be aware of every movement, every action and every detail of what you're doing. Lose yourself in whatever you're doing and try to blank out everything else.

Accept that you can't change the past. No amount of thinking about the past will change the results of wrong decisions made, nor will it bring back those lovely situations you may remember. The sooner you accept this, the faster you will find it easier to live in the present.

When I feel caught up in thinking about the past, I sometimes think of the Lily Tomlin quote: *"Forgiveness means giving up all hope for a better past"*.

Accept that the future is capricious – the future will become the present very soon. However well you plan the future, there are factors beyond your control that will affect the future you've planned. Worrying about getting old, being fired from work, and worrying about your health are all futile exercises, since there is really no way to predict the future. If you can accept this fact, it will be easier for you to enjoy the here and now.

Focus on and count your breath —-focusing on inhaling and exhaling and counting every breath for even a minute or two is a quick and easy way to be in the here and now. As you count every breath you are also becoming conscious of all of your other senses. You are able to see more sharply, hear more clearly, smell and feel the air as it touches your skin.

Tips on How To Savor the Moment

As I've mentioned earlier, savoring the moment, living in the present, "*carpe diem*" or seizing the moment is a skill that needs to be learned. To help you hone your skill, here are tips:

Practice – There is no other way to learn and be a master of the skill of savoring the moment than by practice. At first, it may be difficult and you will catch yourself with your mind wandering. Don't castigate yourself and don't get disheartened – just continue practicing. Practice in the morning, practice as you drive, as you eat and in every chance you get, practice. As you continue to practice, you'll get better.

Here's a fun exercise, start to do things differently. For example, when you are brushing your teeth, stand on one leg, or use the other hand than you usually do. Drive a different way to work. Put your sandwich together differently. All of these things will help you remember to stay in the moment.

For example, I often do a conscious eating practice where after every bite, I put down the spoon and notice chewing my food. It brings me into the moment and I can enjoy the meal more fully.

Be aware of your thoughts – it doesn't matter if your mind wanders as long as you're aware that it's straying or digressing either to the past or the future. Awareness will lead to change. Meditation is a great way to do this – check out my book on Meditation (https://www.amazon.com/Beginning-Meditation-Busy-People-Stressed-ebook/dp/B007MFLOW)

Don't force your thoughts out – as your mind drifts and you're aware of it, don't be too hard on yourself and try to push them out of your head. Once you're aware of the drifting, gradually and gently let it leave and then take yourself back to the present.

Sometimes it's just a matter of taking one deep breath. It can be helpful to post reminders —posting reminders to take one deep breath on the wall or on your fridge, making the reminder as your screensaver or wallpaper for your computer, or asking your partner to remind you every now and then, will help you keep your focus on practicing. Of course when you see the reminder, the practice is to stop, if even for 10 seconds, and take one deep breath and feel yourself returning to your body and being present in the moment.

There will be slip-ups. Don't worry, even with a little practice, you'll notice progress.

Challenge: One of the best ways to be present is to stop multitasking. The challenge for this chapter is to choose one activity that you multi-task with, for example eating in front of the TV or computer, or listening to the radio while you drive, or cleaning your desk while you wait for a computer program to open, and stop. Just take that time to focus on the one task.

For example, if you are eating a meal, then just eat. Focus on your food, noticing and enjoying each bite. If you are driving, just notice yourself in the driver's seat, how it feels.

These short moments of presence will start to bring you back to the moment and you can start to notice how you really feel about your life. This is a critical step for the rest of the book!

CHAPTER 3

2nd Secret to Happiness – Take control of your life

"It isn't until you come to a spiritual understanding of who you are--not necessarily a religious feeling, but deep down, the spirit within--that you can begin to take control." – Oprah Winfrey

With all the uncertainties and madness of this world, being in charge of your life can be very difficult.

What if I tell you that you have more control of your life than you think?

Sure, there are things that you have little control over such as politics and global warming (although you can still take action). But you can control your response. You can control your thoughts, your emotions and your reactions to everything that's happening around you. You are the architect of your life and everything that happens to you is a result of your thoughts, emotions and reactions.

When you're not in control of your life, you drift through life, waiting for circumstances and others to steer your life. You are like a rudderless boat drifting in the ocean, going wherever the tide brings it and usually with disastrous results such as running aground or crashing on the reefs. Sometimes you just drift from dull spot to dull spot. You often end up at the mercy of others. You can become a pawn in someone else's game.

"If it's never our fault, we can't take responsibility for it. If we can't take responsibility for it, we'll always be its victim." – Richard Bach

Many people live their lives this way. It's called 'Being a Victim'.

What is Appealing about Being a Victim?

Being a victim is actually a very comfortable place to live. Many people spend most of their lives here. Why? Here are the top five reasons:

1. *Attention and validation.* When you are a victim and spend your time talking about how the world (or someone specific) has done you wrong, you get a lot of sympathy and support. People pay attention to you and help you out.

2. *Risk avoidance.* When you feel like a victim you tend to avoid taking action, and to risk failure or rejection.

3. *Less responsibility.* When you feel like a victim, responsibility for our actions, beliefs and thoughts is attributed to someone or something else. This way

you don't have to take responsibility for your life, make hard decisions and handle the consequences (good or bad).

4. *You're the right one.* When you feel like a victim, you generally feel right and justified. You are right, they are wrong, and life is simple.

5. *You're in good company.* When you feel like a victim you're in the company of everyone else out there who also feels powerless. Our media and even our families support us being victims. Often when people start to take real responsibility for their own lives and experience, the people around them discourage them from making the change.

6. *You're staying in your comfort zone.* If you stay a victim, you don't have to change. Change can be scary. Our brains are generally pretty comfortable with where we are, even if we are unhappy. But change is scary, so we might think it's best to stay where we are rather than try to change and risk disappointment or things getting worse.

We're very supported by our culture in being victims. As long as you are controlled by external forces, as long as you give responsibility for your happiness to others, you allow them, even invite them to control your experience. As John Holt and Ivan Illich, leaders in educational reform talked about the "hidden curriculum" of our educational system, where years and years of learning the truth from teachers, being taught in the factory model in schools has the hidden agenda of molding us into "compliant consumers" thinking that our happiness is gained from external sources (the new car, the new diet) rather than internally. Easily led to buy or do things that an authority tells them will improve their lives and make them happy.

If you want to take the conspiracy theory to the extreme, it's almost as if our society has created something like the Matrix . Here is a quote from the movie:

> Morpheus continues, "Let me tell you why you're here. You're here because you know something. What you know you can't explain. But you feel it. You've felt it your entire life. That there's something wrong with the world. You don't know what it is, but it's there. Like a splinter in your mind, driving you mad. It is this feeling that has brought you to me. Do you know what I'm talking about?"
>
> With a voice full of uncertainty, Neo asks, "The Matrix?"
>
> "Do you want to know what it is?" Morpheus inquires very deliberately.
>
> At a nod from Neo, Morpheus continues, "The matrix is everywhere. It is all around us. Even now, in this very room. You can see it when you look out your window or when you turn on your television. You can feel it when you go to work, when you go to church, when you pay your taxes. It is the world that has been pulled over your eyes to blind you from the truth."
>
> "What truth?" asks Neo.
>
> "That you are a slave, Neo. Like everyone else you were born into bondage, born into a prison that you cannot smell or taste or touch. A prison for your mind.

As long as we believe "something out there" can make us happy, our happiness is being controlled by other people, maybe people who love us, like our families and communities, or maybe people who want something from us, like advertisers who want to keep us feeling unhappy so we continue to purchase their products.

Enough about conspiracy theories though!!!

The real problem with being a victim is that victims don't tend to be very happy. Happiness goes against the role you are playing. If you are casting yourself into the victim role and then go around being happy all the time, no one will believe you.

So you get to choose. Do you want to be a victim, or do you want to be happy?

Here's a quick exercise that will demonstrate this idea. After you've finished reading the next paragraph, put down the book and give this exercise a try. You can click on this link and follow along on YouTube: https://www.youtube.com/watch?v=QybQfCbazc0

Remember a time when you felt really happy. Remember a specific moment, where you were, who you were with, what was happening. Now really notice that feeling of happiness. Notice where it is in your body. Notice that you can have this feeling right now. It may not be exactly the same as it was, but you can bring it back into your body.

Now put down the book and actually do the exercise above :-)

Notice that even though you were not at the place you remembered, and currently having that experience right now, you were able to bring back that feeling of happiness. So, even without those external trappings, you can have the feeling.

Do you see how that means that the feeling of happiness lives within you? Yes, that location, those people, that situation might have been triggers for the feeling, they might have put you into a state where you chose to feel happy. But the happiness was all yours.

If they had created that happiness, then you would not have been able to experience it again – because it would have been theirs.

But you were able to experience it again. That is because the your feelings are yours. They are generated by you, and you can choose to generate them whenever you want. It might not always be easy, but it is possible.

When big advertising and the people who want to control us and make us "compliant consumers" continue to pressure us to believe that our feelings are controlled externally, it allows them to continue to have power over our thoughts, actions, and happiness.

When we choose to notice that actually our feelings are created internally, then we take control from them, and start to really take control of our own lives, and our own happiness.

What does taking control of your life mean?

"Your time is limited, so don't waste it living someone else's life. Don't be trapped by dogma--which is the result of others' opinions. Don't let the noise of others' thinking drown out your own inner voice, and most important, have the courage to follow your heart and intuition. These somehow already know what you truly want to become. Everything else is secondary." – Steve Jobs

Taking control of your life is another way of describing self-efficacy, or your belief about your ability and capability to influence what happens in your life. If you believe in your abilities and capabilities, you feel and act differently from those who have reservations about their capabilities. You have high aspirations and strong commitments to the goals that you choose to follow. Failure will not inhibit your motivation and you are able to recover your confidence quickly in the face of setbacks.

You take control of your life when you take responsibility for your actions and assume leadership for every aspect of your life. Once you are in control of your life you become a more positive person, you are capable of meeting problems head on and you become a happier person.

It means realizing what you can control, and what you can not. I've realized that many people have the ideas of what they can be responsible for and what they can not upside down.

Here's what I mean. We often think we have no control over things that we actually do have control over – like how we respond to our world. We also think we have control over things we have no control over – like the people around us.

One example from my life is with a dear friend of mine. I really wanted him to be happy. So I did everything I could to "make him happy". I got him work. I cooked him breakfast. I focused on doing everything I could to "make him happy". Why? Because I thought that if I was able to make him happy, he would treat me better, and "make me happy".

Finally, I realized that nothing I could do would make him happy. Happiness is an inside job. I was trying to control him and his happiness, while at the same time being a victim by thinking that he controlled my happiness.

I see this a lot in the people I work with. It comes back to that training we get from the time that we're really little. The training that our internal experience is generated by things in our outside world. So, that means that we can control others, and that we can't control ourselves.

Once we realize that we've got it backwards, life gets a lot easier! Taking responsibility for our own reality has a few benefits:

1. It stops other people from being able to control you.

2. It allows you to create your own reality

3. It takes you off the hook for taking responsibility for other people's reality

When you start doing this, you'll discover that you have more confidence in your destiny. You take control of your life when you take responsibility for your actions and assume leadership for every aspect of your life. Once you are in control of your life you become a more positive person, you are capable of meeting problems head on and you become a happier person.

Why do people find it difficult to take control of their lives?

Usually, the main reason is Fear. Maybe they're afraid to dream, afraid to follow that dream and afraid to achieve that dream because of the fear of failure. Staying in their comfort zone is easier and safer rather than taking a risk. The sad thing is, sometimes they don't even realize that it is this fear that is holding them back from taking control of their lives and reaching their maximum potential.

Limiting beliefs such as "I'm can't do math" or "I'll never be able to talk in front of an audience." "If I apply for that job I really want I'll fail and humiliate myself" are maybe the other reasons why your self-efficacy might be low. These are stories you tell yourself and have nurtured for a long time that they become old habits.

The life story of Steve Jobs is for me the most fitting example of how to take control of your life. Steve Jobs, the technology visionary, charismatic pioneer in computer engineering and most known as CEO and co-founder of Apple Inc. rose to prominence in spite of the overwhelming baggage of his past. He was an unwanted baby that was given up for adoption. He didn't even finish college because of lack of funds. At a young age of 20 he started Apple Inc. with a friend in a garage. He even had to sell his Volkswagen, his most precious possession, to finance the production of the first Apple computer.

After 6 years of success, the business suffered in the face of stiff competition from IBM. The launch of "Lisa," the pair's new creation, was also a fiasco. These setbacks did not dampen Steve's and his partner's zeal and passion to succeed. They came up with the Macintosh, after Steve Jobs reportedly appropriated the project, ruthlessly driving their computer engineers and even flying a pirate flag on top of the building where they worked.

The Mac was a huge success! From a garage, Apple computer grew to be a $2 billion dollar business with more than 4,000 employees only after 10 years.

But it was not all a bed roses for Steve Jobs, because at 30 he was booted out from the company he founded by a guy he, himself, had recruited. He sold his more than $20 million worth of Apple stock, travelled aimlessly in Europe and spent his days biking along the beach feeling lost and sad.

But it was this debacle that set him free "to enter one of the most creative periods of my life", Steve Job's very own words. He considered his being fired from Apple as the best thing that ever happened to him.

In the next five years he founded two companies, NeXTStep & Pixar. NeXTStep didn't do well but Pixar was another success story that made him a billionaire. He went back to Apple, which was then in financial trouble, first as a consultant and later, regained his seat as CEO. Even after he was diagnosed and underwent surgery for cancer of the pancreas, he still drove Apple to new heights, getting the company back on its feet financially and introducing cutting edge technology such as the iPod.

Why was he so successful? Because he took control of his life.

Quotable quotes from Steve Jobs

"Sometimes life hits you in the head with a brick. Don't lose faith."

"You have to trust in something – your gut, destiny, life, karma, whatever. This approach has never let me down, and it has made all the difference in my life. "

"Do you want to spend the rest of your life selling sugared water or do you want a chance to change the world"

"Be a yardstick of quality. Some people aren't used to an environment where excellence is expected"

"We don't get a chance to do that many things, and every one of them should really be excellent because this is our life. Life is brief and then you die, you know? And we've all chosen to do this or that with our lives. So it better be damn good. It better be worth it"

Why does taking control of your life make you a happier person

I was inner tubing in Asheville last week and it made me think about life. In some ways life is like floating down a river. We can't always control what comes into our lives. Sometimes the current is going one way, and we can paddle as hard as we can against the current and still end where the river takes us. Sometimes the chaotic river gives you options and choices; You are what and where you are today because of the choices you've made – good or bad.

You even have a choice of how you respond to the river. Your feelings are not controlled by external factors nor are they controlled by anyone unless you give them permission to take control. When someone is rude and obnoxious to you, you can choose to be angry or opt to react in a more positive way, such as ignoring the obnoxious action. This is often called your option to re-act or to act.

Event + Response = Outcome

When you have control of your life or have a high sense of self-efficacy you can better control events that affect your life. It makes you feel more powerful and feel better about yourself. You look at trials and problems not as threats but as challenges to be mastered. You are more involved and take more interest in activities that will improve your life. When you fail or suffer setbacks you easily bounce back and recover a strong sense of being able to improve what caused the failure. You may blame yourself for not doing what should have been done or doing it poorly, but because you believe that you can conquer your own weaknesses and the challenges of the task, you are confident that you will finally succeed. Believing that you control your life rather than your life controlling you will make you a more fulfilled and happier person.

If you have low self-efficacy or you are not in control of your life, anxiety and depression may set in when you experience setbacks or failure. You may feel hopeless and helpless. This can cause stress that can affect your health and total well-being. It is not the exposure to stressors such as failure that causes stress. It is your lack of faith in your ability to manage these stressors that is so harmful.

They say that *Like Attracts Like*. When you are in control of your life or have a high sense of self-efficacy you tend to seek out and develop social relationships with people who are themselves very much in control. From these people you will learn more how to manage difficult situations and lessen the unpleasant effects of failure to bring you more satisfaction in your life.

How to take control of your life

The good news is, you can learn to take control of your life. You can create or increase your level of self-efficacy one step at a time. It's all a matter of developing an attitude that you practice consistently, first with small things and progress to bigger things, as you become used to being successful in your endeavors. You can face the fears and limiting beliefs that may prevent you from being in control of your destiny.

Tips

Breaking free of limiting beliefs – Since your beliefs form the basis of how you perceive yourself, what you can do and can't do, they necessarily also limit your behavior, whether these beliefs are true or not. As long as you believe them, they will inevitably impact and shape your perceptions and make you less powerful, less in control.

How do these beliefs get formed? Usually they are formed when we are growing up, usually before the age of seven. So someone who is seven years old, with all the life experience and skills of a seven year old, created the beliefs that bind you today, with all the life experience and skills you have now. Isn't it time to make some corrections?

The Power of Belief and Circus Elephants

Circus elephants are huge, powerful creatures, restrained by a tiny rope. How does that work?

When the elephant is young, they tie a rope around its leg and pound the stake into the ground. The baby elephant, being young and unskillful, fights and fights against the rope and is not strong enough to break it and get free. It will sometimes try for days, expending all its energy, until, finally, it stops trying.

The baby elephant learns to believe that the small rope will hold it.

As the elephant grows up, the circus handler makes the loop around its leg larger, BUT uses the same rope! Even as an adult, the elephant never tries to break free. It has learned the "truth". It has formed the belief that that small rope is enough to hold it to that spot.

Many of us are like this elephant. We've learned the "truth" when we were small, and now that we are big and could easily break free of the ideas that bind us, we don't. We don't even try.

Sometimes, the biggest stumbling blocks to taking control of your destiny are the limiting beliefs that are deeply rooted in your psyche such as "I'm not good enough," " I can't do this," "I'm too old" or "I'm too young". You can start to identify, confront and purge out of your life these limiting beliefs to lessen their control over your actions and reactions. You also can understand the triggers that call forth these incapacitating thoughts so that you can be proactive and take a more active role in shaping your life. Find out if there are feelings, actions or situations that trigger these beliefs and learn how to have the feeling, action or situation without calling forth the beliefs.

Exercise – Beliefs and the Scientific Method

1. Take out a sheet of paper (or open a new document on your computer) and write down five things that you believe stand in the way of your happiness. List five experiences you don't want to have.

2. Now write down the kind of beliefs that might lead someone to have these experiences.
3. Notice if any of these beliefs sound familiar, and take a moment to think about whether they are always true. Are there any instances or situations where these beliefs are false?

Once you've identified your limiting beliefs, don't hide from them. Challenge these limiting beliefs and ask yourself what evidence you have that supports them. There are several ways to work with limiting beliefs, and I'm not sure which one will work the best for you. Below is one that has worked for many people.

What is a belief?

A belief is an idea that is supported by evidence. You may have some beliefs that have already changed.

For example, when I started kitesurfing last year, I wasn't very good. I couldn't stand up, I was frustrated a lot, and I wondered if I would ever succeed.

Then, as I practiced, I got better. Now I believe that I'm okay at kitesurfing and have more hope of getting better.

Thus my belief about kitesurfing has changed.

It's helpful to take a belief and really look at the evidence that supports it.

Two illustrative cases.

I once worked with Julia who had the belief that she was not smart enough to start her own business. What was this belief supported by?

1. She had gotten a B– in algebra in high school.

2. Her father had started a business and it had failed, impacting the family's finances.

3. Her guidance counselor had done a job analysis for her and it had indicated other choices were better.

This is pretty compelling evidence! We'll talk more about what happened with Julia shortly. Now, my own personal experience.

In my late teens, I decided I wanted to write. I had been told all my life that I was a bad writer. I had moved to the US in kindergarten and had to take remedial writing. Then in high school I did poorly in writing. In college, again I had to take remedial writing. In my first real job, I asked my boss what I could do to improve myself as an employee, thinking that he would suggest that i learn a new technology. He also sat me down and told me that I was not a very good writer.

Even so, I realized that I had a message that I really wanted to express, so I started writing in collaboration and getting better. This book is one of the things I was called to write.

Steps for Changing Negative Beliefs into Positive Ones

1. First, identify the negative, limiting belief. Generally, the common ones start with "I am…".

For example:

- I am lazy.
- I am unattractive.
- I'm not good enough.
- I'm not worth it.
- I can't do it. (Be specific – what can't you do?)
- I am alone.
- I am too old.
- I am unsuccessful in…

Remember that there are no true or false beliefs, only useful and detrimental ones.

What are the steps?

One thing about a lot of the beliefs that are listed above is that they are not well defined. For example: 'I am not good enough.'

It's very broad and general. If you have beliefs like this, consider asking the next question: 'For what?'

Then you'll get a more well-defined belief, for example: 'I am not good enough to be successful at my own business.'

Again, when we look at this belief, it's still a little general. So we might ask: 'Not good enough at what?'

So then we get an even more well-defined belief, for example: 'I am not good enough at attracting customers to start my own business.'

Write down three limiting beliefs that you might have. Now look at them and start to ask some questions, good questions include:

For what?

At what?

Because? (For example – I am not good enough... because?)

See if you can turn them into well-defined beliefs.

2. Think about what possible value this belief might have in your life. I assume all beliefs started with some value. For example my belief that I was not good at writing stopped me from writing and getting criticized. The value to me was that I really don't like people being angry at me or disappointed, and thinking I was bad at writing stopped that from happening.

My belief that I was not a good writer also helped me to be successful because it got me to hire an editor and to practice and study to become a better writer.

What possible value, either now or in the past did having this belief have for you?

3. Examine the evidence. First write down the evidence.

What is every single thing you can think of that supports this belief? Now let's start looking at it!

Often when you look at the evidence supporting your beliefs closely, you can see some alternative explanations for them that don't necessarily support the belief.

Applying these principles to my friend's case,

a. *She got a B– in high school algebra.* I asked her some questions about this time and found out that she missed two exams because she was very sick that semester. When I asked her how she did in other math classes, she said she did well.

b. *Her father had failed in business.* With some probing I learned that her father had started a highly speculative business with little training. She was thinking of starting a business in a well-established field in which she had a degree.

c. *Her guidance counselor didn't suggest starting a business.* She told me that this was in high school. She is certainly different now than she was then! We went to a couple of websites with job profiles and found that some of them did indicate that she has a great profile for being an entrepreneur.

Once we loosened the grip that the evidence had on her, we started looking for evidence that she would make a good entrepreneur, including that she is well-organized, manages time well, and loves talking to people about her work.

In my case, I love to write and I felt a strong calling to get information out to people in a way that helps them. My belief that I was not a good write helped me to be successful because it made me find the people who could help me do better what I wanted to do. Now I wouldn't say that I'm a great writer. I'm not expecting a Pulitzer prize for my non-fiction works, but I have gotten comments that my books are clear and easy-to-read, which is my goal.

So over time, and with persistence, I have changed that belief!

Try this for yourself.

Look at the evidence that you wrote down, and think about each instance (or if there were a lot of them, think about a representative instance that stands out). See how you can look at that evidence in a new way and start to loosen the grip of the belief.

Now look at the counter-examples. What are some experiences or evidence that you have that does not support the belief?

4. Choose a belief you would like to have instead. The new belief should be something that you carefully crafted and gives you some input. It might not be "People give me money". It might be "I attract money into my life".

The new belief should be positive and something that you can effect. State your new belief out loud three times and see how it feels. Try standing up and taking a step forward as you say it.

5. Now look for evidence for your new belief every day. Even if it's small evidence, the more you start looking for support of your new belief, the more you'll find it!

Put everything you have in overcoming these limiting beliefs and imagine how liberating it will be without them, how much you're capable of doing and what you can attain when you have the new beliefs.

Taking small steps and building on successes – The most effective way to take control of your life is through mastery experiences. This means that you have to perform small tasks that are easy to perform or small challenges that are not so daunting so that success is almost always assured.

Building small successes will bolster your self-efficacy and will give you confidence to meet bigger challenges. Setbacks or failure could undermine your efforts to take control of your life but because these are only small setbacks, they won't succeed in discouraging you.

In fact you need these small setbacks, since if at all times you're met with success, you could end up looking forward to speedy and easy results. Then when you are met with more substantive failure you may be really discouraged. Once you're satisfied that you have more control over your destiny, you will persist when faced with hardships and bounce back from setbacks.

Tips on how to build small successes

Look forward to experiencing success and learning from your mistakes – Anticipate success. When you're met with failure don't focus on what went wrong, focus on what could be done to have a more positive outcome.

Be positive – When you're met with setbacks, don't allow negative thoughts to control you. Adopt the attitude that you still have an opportunity to make it right. Concentrate on the next turn and don't get stalled by negativity.

Practice – When you are successful, notice what made you attain that success and do it again, fast. This means you continue to practice until you perfect the art.

Celebrate – Celebrate your successes by rewarding yourself. What you celebrate is replicated, because the more you celebrate the more successes you will make.

When you take control of your life, you are much more the captain of your ship and the master of your destiny. If you are persistent, no one else will determine what your life will be or how you'll live your life – you will.

CHAPTER 4
3rd Secret to Happiness – Act as if

"Act as if you were already happy and that will tend to make you happy" – Dale Carnegie

Act as if you're rich, act as if you're healthy, act as if you're happy, act as if you already have what you wish for or act as if you know how to do something, even if you don't yet.

'Act as If' something is already happening in your life even if it's not, or at least, not yet. 'Act as If' you can't fail.

'Acting as If' is actually creating a situation for all these to become true in your life.

When you "Act as If', both your conscious and unconscious minds are involved in creating the circumstances that will make things happen. 'Acting as If' sends powerful directives to your subconscious mind to come up with resourceful and innovative ways to attain your goals. When you "Act as If" you'll start to be more conscious and attentive to things that will make you achieve your goal.

Many books have been written and even movies made espousing this concept and at first I thought it was all hogwash. Not anymore, I can assure you--it works. It's working for me and it will work for you.

What does "Act as If" Mean

"Acting as If" is actually taking a leap of faith. It is the act of believing in or acknowledging something that doesn't exist yet. There may not even be signs or indications that it will come. It is choosing to live with an unshakable confidence in the things unseen, without evidence or proof and with no guarantees.

Here's some research that might help understand this concept. At any moment your unconscious mind can process about 2,000,000 pieces of information. Your conscious mind can only process about 40,000 pieces of information.

This is like there being sixteen movies running at the same time, BUT you can only watch one of them. How do you figure out which one to watch?

Your system must have some simple sorting mechanism to decide which pieces of information are important to you and which are not important.

The system that is used to make these decisions is the Reticular Activating System (RAS). It's the filter that decides which pieces of information come into your consciousness, and which do not.

How does your RAS know what is important? It filters based on who you think you are, your identity, values, beliefs, habits, and survival needs.

One of the goals of the RAS is to support your current beliefs. For example, if you believe in intuition and have a sense of how you receive intuitive guidance, your RAS will be sorting for that type of data. If you think people are generally good and do nice things, then your system will be sorting for that data as well, and things that do not support that belief will be filtered out.

It's hard to imagine that there is that much information out there that we are missing every second. Once you start to accept it, you can see the power of challenging your beliefs and setting your life up to see things a new way – a happier way.

Most people subscribe to the conviction that "to see is to believe". However, this actually limits your experience and repudiates the power of your mind and your imagination. It holds you back from creating new experiences that will expand your horizon, and prevents you from being a better and happier person.

What happens if you shift that thought to "to believe is to see"?

For some, the concept of "Acting as If" is essential to their lives. For others it is something new and worth trying and for many, it's an idea that is arcane or cryptic.

No matter how you relate to this concept, the truth is, at some point in your life you may have experienced the power of 'Acting as If" without giving it a name.

"Acting as If" is comparable to the concept of "you get exactly what you expect". Both are very potent concepts and can help you be happier, if only you live being aware of them and allow them to influence your life. Rather than waiting for things to happen or wishing for something or merely allowing events and circumstances to influence how you feel, why don't you act as if you already have everything around you or within you that will make you more fulfilled, successful, and happy, which in truth, you already do!

Why "Acting as If" makes you a happier person?

Happiness does not happen by accident nor is it something you achieve through good luck. It is something that needs to be cultivated. It is a state of mind that does not depend on the size of your bank account or your status in society. Your state of well-being or happiness will depend on your choice; if you choose to be happy, you will be happy. Usually, you need to use the power of your mind to create happiness and "acting as if" is using the power of your mind, both your conscious and subconscious minds.

Acting as if you're happy, even if you don't feel particularly cheerful, can raise your spirits and change your mood. Feeling happy makes you smile, while feeling sad makes you frown. BUT this relationship between emotion and behavior is a two way street. Behavior can also bring about emotion. Acting as if you're happy by smiling can make you feel happy.

"Acting as If" keeps you centered in your aspirations. It keeps you convinced in its manifestation and eliminates doubt. 'Acting as If' also increases faith and belief. It even convinces your subconscious into acknowledging with certainty what you want to be or what you aspire for. If you act as if you're happy by doing what happy people do, such as smiling, laughing, being appreciative of what you have and savoring life's joy, then you'll be happy.

How do you 'Act as If'

Acting as if starts with imagining that what you want to happen has already come to pass.

I've learned a few tricks to this through studying a lot and trying this out myself.

1. *'Act as If' right where you are.* You want to act as if you already have what you want, and experience the feelings of that experience. So for example, if you want a great job, act as if the job you already have is great, expect it to be great, look for ways that it is great. Surprisingly enough, this can actually change your job. Either your job will conform to your expectations, or you'll find yourself with a new job.

2. *Take Right Action.* Be careful of making commitments with 'Act as If'. For example, acting as if you have $1,000,000 does not mean running up your credit cards expecting the money to show up. Acting as if you've lost three dress sizes might mean buying a beautiful dress in that size that fits your budget. It doesn't mean buying a whole new wardrobe.

3. *Take action.* I heard a cute story about this. A Rabbi was standing at a bus stop when a young woman ran up huffing and puffing to catch the bus. Once they were sitting on the bus she asked the Rabbi, "You have a connection with spirit, when you are late for the bus do you pray that you'll catch it?". The Rabbi replied, "I pray, and I also run." The meaning here is that Acting as If' you have what you want can make possible the opportunity for you to take action. 'Acting as If' you have the perfect job might just put the perfect job into your line of sight. You do have to apply for it!

The more energy and passion you devote to "Acting as If", the faster you will realize your aspirations, the quicker you'll become what you want to be. It is important to persist in 'Acting as If'. The more you act this way, the closer you will move into the reality of what you want to be. Before long, you won't be pretending anymore because you will be the realization of your vision.

So, how do you pretend to be happy? How do actors portray a happy character? Put yourself in the shoes of an actor, and pretend that you're acting out the role of a happy person. Acting as if you're happy will make you happy.

See yourself as a happy person. Look at that person and assume the persona of that person; see what they see, feel how they feel, act how they act and be who they are. Dwell in your vision. Keep pretending or acting as if it's real. Convince yourself that you're happy and by doing so you'll also convince the people around you.

Exercise: Smiling

Here's a quick exercise to try for 2 minutes every day. I do it and it changed my life. It's so simple you might be tempted to ignore it. Please don't. Actually, try it right now. Put down the book and smile!

Smile for 2 minutes a day. Set a timer, or do it to your favorite song in the car, or when you are getting dressed. Choose 2 minutes a day and lift the corners of your mouth for those two minutes and notice how you feel. You don't have to feel happy. It doesn't need to be a "genuine" smile (although that will be more fun). Just lift the corners of your mouth.

You could, in addition, choose to smile more every day. Smile at people in the mall. Notice how it changes your life. I think you'll be surprised!

CHAPTER 5

4th Secret to Happiness – Don't take anything personally

"No one can make you feel inferior without your permission."
– Eleanor Roosevelt

Do you think your abusive boss is zeroing in on you? Do you feel devastated when you hear critical or belittling comments from coworkers or even from a complete stranger? Or, do you get distressed by all the negative news that you see on television? You must be a very unhappy person if you allow all these to adversely affect you.

The 4th secret to happiness is, don't take anything that happens around you personally. Whatever other people do is not because of you. It's because of Them. When you allow what others do or say affect you, you're giving them power over you. We all live in our own minds; we all have our own dreams and lives. When you allow what others say or do affect you, you're assuming that they know what's in your mind and you're allowing them to enter your world.

This is easier to say than to do. When we've been trained all our lives to look outside ourselves for affirmation, we get very sensitive to feedback. It takes real practice for some people to get into the habit of not being strongly affected by what others say and do.

For example, a friend went out on a date with a man who in the first five minutes of the date let her know that they would not be a good match because she was more heavy-set than he was attracted to. What she heard was "You're too fat!". She was enraged. Why? Because it echoed some feeling or belief that she has about herself. It triggered an internal feeling that maybe was created through judgement or rejection. At this point though, she had internalized this feeling that she was too fat. The messengers were so good at telling her that "truth", that she started telling it to herself.

Hogwash, you might say, but here's the other side of the story. The next week she went on a date with a man who very politely let her know that he tended to like women who were more heavy-set. What she heard was "You're too thin!" She experienced this statement completely differently. Her attitude was "Oh, that's his choice." My hypothesis is that she experienced the "You're too thin" comment differently because it didn't resonate for her. Not one part of her believed that she was too thin, so she let it go.

Exercise:

Try this out for yourself.

1. Here are some common beliefs that people hold:

    I am too fat for people to think me attractive.

    I am not educated enough (or too well-educated) to get that job.

    I am too dark skinned to be accepted.

    Or think of your own "I'm too X to get Y" phrase. Everyone has them.

2. Now try them out for yourself. Say each one to yourself and rate how it would feel if someone said that to you on a scale of 1–10.

3. Now try on the other side of the continuum. So if you were imagining someone saying that you are too fat, now imagine someone saying that you are too thin. Rate that on a scale of 1–10 and notice the difference.

You'll be a happier person if you don't take things personally!

What does not taking anything personally mean?

Not taking anything personally means not letting anything external to you affect your thoughts and your actions. The opinions of your friend, your boss, your partner or of a complete stranger are just that, opinions. They will only become true when you give them credence by believing in them and reacting to them. Whatever harsh or sweet words are thrown to you are not really about you, BUT about whomever it is that's saying those words and based on their own issues. There is no way you can control what others will do, say, or think BUT you have control over how you will react.

Not taking thing personally really has two faces: what they say, and how you interpret it.

Let's take that apart a little.

What they say.

We see other people through our own filters and experience. They make snap judgments about who you are based on what is going on in their own heads. It's almost like being an actor in a movie. Each person we know sees us in a different role. They see us playing different parts. If we've known each other a long time, they might have seen more of our parts and get a broader sense of who we are, but still they are responding not to us – but to their story of who we are.

I just watched *Superman*, the movie from 1978 with Christopher Reeves. In the movie Clark Kent was able to fool everyone into thinking he was a bumbling news reporter and not noticing that he looked exactly like Superman. That's because people were seeing what they expected to see. When he was Clark Kent, they noticed his hesitancy and his bumbling, and not his big strong shoulders, square jaw, blue eyes and black hair. As superman, it wasn't just the cape and the glasses, it was that he was able to project a completely different persona. And people believed it.

For another example, take Meryl Streep. In *The Devil Wears Prada*, she played Miranda, a demanding boss, and in *Mama Mia!* she plays Donna, a sweet villa owner. If I were interacting with Miranda from the *The Devil Wears Prada* character, I'd do it in a very different way than I would Donna.

This is an extreme example, and the point is that we have a sense of who we are, we might think we are nice, or sweet, or hard, or difficult, or that we have different roles at work and at home and on the golf course based on our own experience of ourselves. Other people also see us both through their filters, and through their limited experience of us. Maybe they've just seen us as a demanding boss, or as a sweet villa owner.

Their response is going to be based on what they know of us, which generally isn't much.

So when you take their response personally, it's not really fair to either of you. You are getting a response based on a role that maybe you sometimes occupy (or maybe you just remind them of someone who does).

How you interpret it.

You are creating a story about what is going on between you.

There are lots of reasons why someone's communication might make you upset. Perhaps:

- they really were trying to put you down

- they have a headache

- in their culture that's how they communicate with everyone

- they are feeling stressed

- they are responding to your communication style

When someone communicates with you, you get to decide which of these filters you choose to interpret their actions. You could choose to think that they are trying to put you down or insult you, or you could choose to consider that they might be stressed, or have a headache, or any number of other options. Which of these interpretations do you think will make you happier?

What else could this mean?

A great question to ask when you feel offended by someone or upset by a communication is: What else could this mean? Asking this question will get your brain off of the track of being annoyed at their behavior and onto the track of thinking about ways to be okay or happy with their behavior.

Not taking anything personally is not only not allowing yourself to be affected by the negative things or words thrown at you. It also means not basing your sense of self worth on positive things said about you. If you do, you'll forever depend on others to tell you how great or intelligent or pretty you are. When you don't get that affirmation from others, then you can lose your sense of self-worth.

Not taking anything personally is being centered and grounded and knowing that only you can determine your destiny, your course of action and your way of thinking. It means a strong self-awareness and a realization that you cannot control what others will do or say, and you have 100% control of your response. When people treat you unkindly or cruelly, admonish yourself that your response is your choice, and then choose a response that will leave you your self-respect and dignity.

Why not taking things personally makes you a happier person

What the concept of not taking anything personally gives you is freedom. You are free to choose happiness regardless of what is happening around you. It also gives you freedom to let other people's actions and comments roll off your back effortlessly. Not taking anything personally frees you from pointless resentment and pain and also frees you from feeling unnecessarily responsible for how other people feel when they take your actions personally.

The more you don't take things personally, the happier you will be. Of course there will be times when you will still feel hurt or affected BUT not without reason. The effect of not taking things personally is that you are more able to maintain your sense of balance over actions and situations that are not under your control. When you don't take things personally, more often you'll feel good and happy.

How not to take anything personally

The concept of not taking things personally may be easy to understand and for some people it may be a little difficult to apply. Years of conditioning have accustomed us to react to everything that is happening around us and to comments thrown at us especially if the comments come from people in authority or from those we respect. Not taking things personally may be difficult to do, and I assure you, very doable. Here's how:

- Understand that you are not the center of the universe and are only a bit player in the drama of other people's lives. Get rid of the "I-me-myself" notion and you can view everything in the right context. Once you do, you'll be clearer-headed and can choose to react accordingly.

- Give everyone the benefit of the doubt. Ask the question: What else could this mean? And see what answers come up in your brain. Just pause for a second before reacting and wonder if maybe the person said something negative because they were not feeling well, or had a bad day.

- Choose your response. Remind yourself that you can't control what others do or say, and you are in complete control of how you'll respond, and that is refusing to believe what has been said about you.

- Don't dwell on the situation and instead re-focus your attention on something else. Notice if this person treats other people the same way.

- Try to feel compassion for the other person; they may be very unhappy. Compassion won't weaken you and it may will even make you feel better.

- Learn to speak up and communicate in a non-combative manner. For all you know the other person does not even realize that their words or actions are causing you grief.

Exercise:

This exercise will help you get to the underlying beliefs behind being sensitive to certain interactions.

1. Think back to the last time you got really upset about something that someone said or did in relationship to you. Perhaps a time you felt criticized or put down.

2. Really feel into your response. Notice how you interpreted the information. What did that person's communication say to you about:

   a.   Who they are

   b.   Who you are

   c.   Your value to them

   d.   Your value to yourself

   e.   Your value in the world

3. Ask yourself "What does this mean about me"? And notice what you learn.

What I've learned from this exercise is that I get most impacted when people do things that make me tell myself that I am not worthwhile. That's traditionally been one of my key sore points. It might be completely different from yours. If you do really dig into this exercise though, you'll gain one of the keys that will allow you to take back control of your responses because you can see how it's really reflecting a conversation you are having with yourself. And that is a conversation you can change.

Of course sometimes we get a response about what we ourselves have done or said that disappoints us. Then we may wish to treat this data as useful feedback. Have we been misunderstood? Did we misunderstand the requirements of the other person? Here we can ask for clarification, not taking the signals we receive as statements about who we are, but the expectations of the other person. This can sometimes turn an unpleasant experience into an opportunity for improve our relationships.

CHAPTER 6

The 5th Secret to Happiness – Be an optimist

"A pessimist sees the difficulty in every opportunity; an optimist sees the opportunity in every difficulty" – Winston Churchill

Optimism is looking at a glass as half full rather than half empty. It is believing that when a door closes, another door will open. It may be raining today but tomorrow the sun will shine. Optimism is the sum total of the first four secrets to happiness. You are an optimist when you savor the moment or live in the present and when you are in control of your life. When you're the type of person who can fake it until you make it, or who acts as if everything they desire is already theirs, and when you don't take things personally, then you are an optimist.

Here's a story I love…

Once a traveler was walking along a long road in a strange country.

Along the way he stopped and chatted with some villagers in a field. He asked them, "I'm on the way to the village ahead, can you tell me about it?"

A wise villager asked the man where he had come from.

The man said, "I come from the big village in the mountains."

The wise villager said "What was it like?"

"Horrible!" the man exclaimed, "the people were pushy, the food was gamey, and the weather was miserable."

"I think you will find the next village is much the same," the villager said.

A few hours later another traveler passed by and stopped and asked the wise villager, "I'm on my way to the village ahead, can you tell me about it?"

The wise villager asked him where he had come from.

"I come from the village in the mountains."

"What was it like?", the villager asked.

"Amazing!" the man replied, "the people were really engaging, the food was interesting and different from anything I've ever had, and the weather was really hot and muggy so I got a chance to really experience the local conditions. It was one of the best experiences of my life!"

"I think you will find the next village is much the same," the villager said.

What is optimism?

The definition of optimism by The Online Free Dictionary is "a tendency to expect the best possible outcome or dwell on the most hopeful aspects of a situation".

You are an optimist when you look for something good to come out of a bad situation or use the situation to become a better person. You are an optimist if you face a problem head on, plan a line of attack and stay focused on the solution.

Optimism creates confidence. The true optimist is one who believes they can make success happen through hard work and persistence while employing a plan of action and applying the best strategies to achieve the goal.

It is unrealistic optimism if you believe that success will fall into your lap like a ripe fruit without any effort on your part. Positive thinking alone will not help you overcome obstacles. You are a true or realistic optimist if you acknowledge the need for a serious plan or strategy to overcome the obstacles. Even the process of planning and strategizing will boost your confidence in your own power to succeed.

Understanding the reality that there will be obstacles on the road to success will bring about greater success since it will compel you to take action. If you are convinced that you will succeed and just as convinced that success won't come easy, you'll work harder, plan better even before difficulties arise and persevere longer in the face of obstacles, just like the little engine that could. (*I think I can; I think I can; I thought I could; I thought I could.*)

Why practice optimism

Being an optimist will allow you to pursue your aspirations in life in a more positive way; to dream bigger and better dreams that you can strive to attain. This is not the only advantage of being an optimist.

Here are the reasons why you should practice optimism:

- If you are optimist you are more likely to find the positives from each and every experience. Even when you're faced with obstacles, you will be able to concentrate on the positive aspects that can be extracted from almost all situations.

- When you practice optimism you focus on the lessons learned from past mistakes during the unavoidable setbacks in life so that you don't make the same mistakes again.

- When you practice optimism you will achieve more. This is because you will have a tendency to persevere when faced with hardships. Two of the most outstanding characteristics of optimists are determination and persistence, the biggest factors that contribute to success. As a realistic optimist you are very much aware that success does not come easy, and to be successful you also realize that conviction and determination will help you overcome the temporary setbacks.

- When you practice optimism you will be a healthier person. Studies have shown that optimists are less prone to stress and are therefore not as susceptible to cardiovascular disease and other illnesses caused by stress such as depression, high cholesterol, high blood pressure and the like. Since mind and body are interconnected, the positive influence of the mind conveys positive influence on the functions of the body. Optimism is the foundation of good health.

When you practice optimism, your energy level is higher, and you become more creative and happier person.

Ways to practice optimism

If you want to be an optimist, you can practice some techniques or habits to develop optimism. At the start, practicing optimism may take focus, but as you persevere, they will become second nature to you.

Habits you need to practice to develop optimism

Practice thought awareness. – Thought awareness means discerning your thoughts and identifying them. When you perceive a negative thought, recognize it for what it is, evaluate it, and then release it and let it go.

Practice noticing negative self-talk – If you find yourself worrying about something you have no control over, instead, focus on the positive side of a situation. Ask yourself: "How could this go well?"

Practice directing your energies on situations that you can control and ignore those that you can't.

Practice drawing on positive affirmations – You can practice optimism by using positive affirmations. List simple and clear positive affirmations and place them in locations where you can see them such as on the monitor of your computer, on the door of your refrigerator, on your bathroom mirror or wherever you can be reminded every day. Say them out loud and note your tone of voice. Do you sound doubtful? If so make your tone more assured. You can make use of the following affirmations:

- I am achieving my goals
- I'm in control of my life
- I'm good at what I do
- I am overcoming all obstacles
- I choose to have a positive attitude towards life
- I am becoming who I want to be

Look for the evidence that what you want is coming into existence. Practice seeing only what is good, thinking only good things and acting good all the time.

Practice visualizing the kind of life that you want to have. Draw a picture of how you want your life to be in your mind and set it down on paper. Do you want to have your own business? Do you want to lose 20 lbs and have a fabulous body? Do you want to be known as a loving and caring person? Do you want to be a respected person in your community? Visualize the new person and new life that you want to have and write down your goals. Every day, read what you've written and try it on so that you won't lose sight of your goals. Again, reading aloud is known to be very helpful.

Practice finding joy in even the most mundane of things. Find joy in the rain or in a bright sunny morning, the smile of a complete stranger, the tail wagging of your dog to welcome you home, the smell of freshly brewed coffee, in washing dishes and in every little thing that you experience.

Practice counting your blessings. Write down a gratitude list every night to remind you of all the blessings and the good things that have happened in your life, however small or insignificant they are. This will give you a lift and help you have a more positive outlook in life. Find the song "I am so blessed" on the web and learn it. It is one of the most powerful Western 'mantras' I know.

CHAPTER 7

6th Secret to Happiness – Love yourself

"You yourself, as much as anybody in the entire universe, deserve your love and affection." – Buddha

In our culture, we are continually reminded that before we can love anyone or have a fulfilling life we need to love ourselves first. Songs you hear over the radio and television programs and movies carry this message. Even the internet and print media also reiterate self- love as the key to happiness.

You and I and every one of us, have a loving core within us. Unfortunately, negative messages and experiences bury these feelings deep within us. We grow up to believe that the only way to have love is to receive love from others. This belief leads to a conditional love that brings about an unhealthy dependence of one person on another and eventually, to unhappiness. In truth, love springs from the very core of our being, a love that that is free to be experienced and shared with all.

Self-love is one of the secrets to happiness. As you learn to love yourself, you release all the negativity and pessimism that bury the essence of love in your very being.

To learn to love yourself more deeply, you need to eliminate the hindrances to self-love that have buried that loving core within you. These are:

- Unloving thoughts – Condemnation, censure and judgment whether directed to yourself or to others, arise from an unloving place. Decide to let go of these unloving thoughts and start focusing on tolerance, kindness and acceptance of yourself and of others.

- Negative emotions of the past – Choose to release the negative emotions of the past. Sometimes, we tend to bury our self-love by re-living negative emotions of past experiences. Learn from the lessons of the past, forgive if you have to and go on to the present where the promise of love and happiness exist.

Exercise:

There is a Loving Kindness meditation at www. AngelicoBooks.com/Happy that you can download and listen to every day that will help you to start shifting negative thoughts.

What is self-love exactly?

The other term for self-love is self-esteem. It is acceptance and being comfortable with the four facets of your being: spiritual, physical, cognitive and social. It is being appreciative of your own importance and self-worth, acting responsibly and being accountable towards yourself and others.

Self-love means to accept yourself as you are and to acknowledge the facets of your character that you can't change. To love yourself means to have an unconditional self-acceptance, self-respect and a positive self-image.

But self-love doesn't mean arrogance, conceit and a belief that you're better than others. It means acknowledging that you're not perfect and that you too have weaknesses and that's okay. We are all human.

Self-love means feeling good about yourself and having a healthy self-respect. You know that you're special and unique and that you have your own abilities and talents to offer to the world. To be able to appreciate yourself, it is your responsibility to determine what makes you special and unique and to further cultivate those talents.

Self-esteem or self-love is the value you place on your beliefs about yourself. What determines the value you place on yourself as a human being is how you feel about yourself as well as how you see yourself. It does not mean that you see yourself as perfect, since self-worth comes with the realization that you do make mistakes sometimes. You value yourself mistakes notwithstanding, since you are aware that everyone makes mistakes. You are not what you do. Being able to accept your limitations and weaknesses, and striving to improve and correct such shortcomings are the initial steps to developing self-love.

Positive beliefs are important to self-love. You are uniquely beautiful, lovable and capable. Hidden in your cosmic untapped potentials are intrinsic decency, fundamental human value and inconceivable possibilities. You have a core of strength, wisdom and beauty within you that is worthy of your self-love.

The amount of self-love you express hinges on the choices you make. Incredible potentials rest within your inner core, waiting to be tapped and explored. You may opt to feel guilt over your failings and shortcomings and blame yourself for them or you may choose to uphold yourself because of your good traits. Each choice you make will either promote your self-love or self-esteem or hinder its expression.

Why is self-love a secret to happiness?

Self-love is a key to happiness. If you have a high level of self-esteem or a large dose of self-love you are better equipped to deal with the challenges of life. Consequently, you're more fulfilled, confident, content and victorious. You're probably also a healthier person. Studies show that people who have a healthy dose of self-love are immunized against anxiety and depression that can cause a multitude of illnesses.

Your capacity to love yourself and in the process, love others, can give you a sense of purpose and profound contentment and joy. You will also find pride and fulfill-ment in work-related successes and in your relationship with the people around you – partner, children, family, friends, subordinates or bosses at work and neighbors. If you have a high regard for yourself, smiling at a complete stranger will come naturally, attracting more people to you and widening your range of influence.

Self-love or self esteem is important for two reasons. First, you are inclined to constantly act according to your feeling and beliefs about yourself. If you believe something is true, you will act as though it were in fact true. Second, your opinion of the world around you is affected by your self-esteem or self-love; it acts as a smokescreen that could warp our view of the world.

I really noticed this the other day when I was visiting with my friend Gene. We were lounging at the beach on a lazy Sunday afternoon and I heard him mutter to himself "I'm so lazy, I should get up and do something produc-tive". He looked really unhappy as he said it. I remembered that I used to wake up every morning with those kinds of negative thoughts, and as I was slowly able to transform them to positive thoughts, I became a whole lot happier.

It is only when you love yourself that you can love others. Your capacity to love and be loved can give you purposefulness and fulfillment.

Taking care of yourself as expression of self-love

Taking care of yourself is a physical expression of self-love. Unfortunately, some of us feel that taking care of ourselves is a luxury and something that we'll do if and when we have the time for it, or can afford it, and most of the time we become so busy taking care of others that we finally end up not taking care of ourselves.

Do you remember that on airlines the directions are to put on your own oxygen mask before assisting others? Why do they say this? Because in order to help others, you need to be taken care of first. In order to support others consistently, you need to first look to your own needs. Intellectually, you know you have more to give if you gave to yourself first.

You are entitled to feel good about yourself. It can be very difficult to feel good about yourself when you are suffering from stress or symptoms of ill health because you don't take care of yourself. When you do, it's easy to be drawn into a downward spiral towards a low self-esteem. Listen to what your body, your heart and your mind is telling you. Pay heed to your own needs and wants. If your body is telling you that you've been working too hard, take a break, rest. If you devote time to taking care of yourself, you will realize that you feel good about yourself.

Some acts of self-care for a healthy body include eating healthily, getting enough sleep, exercising, self-pampering such as having a massage or hot oil treatment, undergoing an annual medical examination to ensure that you're healthy. For your emotional, mental and spiritual health, take time to do things you love. Maybe it's listening to music, playing a musical instrument, doing yoga, reading inspirational books, or going fishing, You can also improve your self-esteem by being with people that appreciate you, make you laugh, and who have a positive disposition. Their positive attitude can be infectious and help you develop your own self-esteem.

Taking care of yourself with healthy diet and exercise

A healthy diet combined with exercise will make you feel good mentally and physically and most likely make you feel good about yourself. You can do regular exercise in a gym, walk, jog, bike, swim or even just take the stairs rather than the elevator. Exercise and a healthy diet will help lessen the risk of developing health issues such as heart disease, cancer, diabetes and high blood pressure. They can also provide your body with energy, boost your mood and help you to think clearly.

Taking care of yourself by freeing yourself of stress

Stress has become a major epidemic in our society today. Unfortunately, most, if not all, of us are susceptible to it. Stress hits you where you're most defenseless– your brain and your body. Breaking the stress cycle by taking care of yourself is one way to reclaim your life and become a happier person.

But stress is not all bad. Stress is your body's normal reaction to the threatening or upsetting events that you encounter. When you perceive a menace or danger, your body's defense system automatically reacts in what is known as a stress response - preparing us either to fight or run away.

When your stress response is working properly, it serves as your protection. It keeps you alert, active and focused. During emergencies it can even save your life. It gives you presence of mind and at times, even herculean strength to protect yourself. Your stress response also helps you to overcome challenges. Stress makes you super charged and keeps you focused when studying for an exam or competing in a sport. But after a certain point, it ceases to be beneficial and begins to damage your temper, your health, your efficiency, your relationships, and eventually, the quality of your life.

Harmful stress – signs and symptoms

But how do you know if your stress response has already reached a harmful level? Different people experience stress in different ways. Your capacity to tolerate stress is based on several factors: your outlook in life, your emotional health, your intelligence and even genetics. Your awareness to the fact that you have reached a dangerous stress level is very crucial to your mental and physical health. Stress can be treacherous; it can creep up on you until you become unconscious of it and unaware of how strong an effect it is having on you.

Some of the signs and symptoms that will alert you that your stress level has reached a harmful level:

Physical symptoms – aches & pains; recurring colds; rapid heartbeat; chest pain; high blood pressure, dizziness and nausea; and loss of sex drive, difficulty sleeping and insomnia

Emotional symptoms – depression; restlessness; feeling of isolation and loneliness; mood swings; feeling snowed under; bad temper

Cognitive symptoms – lack of focus; negativism; anxiety; poor judgment; memory problem; endless worrying

Behavioral symptoms – eating and sleeping disorder; substance abuse; isolating oneself from others; procrastination; abandoning responsibility.

These signs and symptoms are also symptoms of other illnesses. The best way to make sure what's causing these symptoms is to consult a doctor.

How to deal with stress

You can free yourself from stress by learning how to deal with it. There are a lot of things you can do to lessen the effect of stress in your life and deal with its symptoms.

Manage your stress. Even if you feel that the stress you feel is uncontrollable, your response to it is something that *is* under your control. Managing stress means taking control – controlling your emotions, your thoughts, your environment, your schedule and the way you handle problems. It also involves changing a stressful condition when you can, and if you can't change the condition, change your response to it.

Learn to relax – Learning some relaxation techniques is one way to control how stress affects you. This could include yoga, deep breathing, stretching, mindful meditation, muscle relaxation and other relaxing ways that will trigger the relaxation response of your body. This can successfully fight stress and alleviate tension.

Learn immediate stress release. At the very instant that you notice stress creeping in, there are several ways you can practice to release this stress. First you must recognize the stressors and then keep a tight rein on your response as stress builds. Quick stress-busting practices using one or more of your senses such as your sense of taste, sight, touch, sound or movement will swiftly sooth your nerves and invigorate you. Take a moment now and think about what soothes you. Do you like beautiful sights? Do soft sounds or music help you relax? How about tasting something delicious? Do you just need a hug? Now, next time you are stressed out, take a moment to stretch and do the activity that most soothes you. Use of the large muscles are great stress relievers. A few pushups of knee bends can do wonders as quick stress relievers. I often will go for a walk in nature if I'm feeling stressed.

Exercise – Regular exercise reduces the symptoms associated with stress, anxiety and depression since it boosts your self-confidence. It also makes you sleep better, and improves your overall sense of well-being and your health. Physical activity also aid in boosting the production of endorphins, the 'feel good' neurotransmitter of your brain. Through exercise, you also cast off stress and tension with your rhythmic movement and physical exertion. As you focus on the exercise, you also start to become more optimistic, and to stay clear headed and calm.

CHAPTER 8

7th Secret to Happiness – Connect with your soul

Your soul is your very core, the essence of your being, and it operates within you providing your most profound intuition and self-knowledge. Your soul is your "Inner Power." It is where the genuine depth of who you really are lives. In your soul lies all the power and might that you need to face and overcome the challenges of life with confidence. Your soul is also a wise and infallible teacher.

Your soul is your link to your God, the Higher Power, the Absolute Truth , the Cosmos or Universe or whatever name you give Him (or Her or It). The secret of your existence, your reason for being, is hidden in your soul. Connecting with your soul will help you in your quest for happiness. If you don't believe in a Higher Power or god, this can be a link to your deep inner self, your core, your essence.

As an extension of the Highest Power, your soul is always in a state of abiding peace, happiness, awareness and perpetual health. You may not acknowledge this consciously, and you innately know deeply that this abiding peace and happiness lies within you.

As you search for success, health, and happiness in this world, you may be unaware of how close you are to genuine success, health and happiness because you're not inward-looking. However, as the weakness of your physical body and the deficiencies of the material world become clear to you, you will experience a spiritual restlessness that sets in motion your desire to communicate with your soul.

Usually a crisis in life awakens spiritual restlessness – the loss of a loved one, a huge financial loss, a close brush with death that makes you face your own mortality. Spiritual restlessness is also sometimes awakened when you reach the pinnacle of success, achieve your goals, gain wealth and fame and still you feel empty and unfulfilled. Fortunate are those whose spiritual restlessness is awakened and who are embarked on spiritual growth and development.

What does connecting with your soul mean?

Do you know that your soul is always striving to connect with you? It communicates with you by way of your deepest desires. Without your being aware of it, it's your soul that drives and motivates you. Unfortunately, the seeming urgencies and activities of the material world drown the inner voice that calls to you. Connecting with your soul means tapping or delving into your true self and understanding your mission on this planet.

When you still your thoughts and open your senses to hear the wisdom of your body, that, itself, is connecting with your soul. Being disconnected to your body and your emotions makes it more difficult for you to listen to your soul. The physical stress and emotional anxiety stored in your body and mind - the sadness, anger, guilt, shame and fear are discordant voices that hinder you from hearing and acknowledging that small inner voice.

Connecting with your soul means willingness to confront and liberate these discordant voices in your body and mind. The better you connect, the more you will regain those delightful feelings of joy, love and spiritedness, and the more you will be able to connect to your "Inner Power". Regardless of how deep your pain is, your soul has the power to heal it. However abandoned or isolated you may feel, you're never really alone – you have your Inner Power. Actually, It has you and is only awaiting for to turn toward It.

Why is connecting with your soul a secret to happiness

We are forever searching for happiness outside of ourselves. Books, magazines, movies, and TV programs are full of our perpetual search for happiness. Little do people know that happiness resides in their very core. Learning to connect with your soul will bring you the most complete happiness you will ever experience.

When you're connected with your soul, your self-love will be heightened, since it will reveal the unique and wonderful person that you really are. Being connected with your soul also gives you a deeper sensitivity that will make you a more loving and kinder person. This will bring about a more satisfying and positive relationship with your partner, your friends, your colleagues at work and with everyone who crosses your path. You'll learn to appreciate other people in a more profound way and become more open, humane and responsive towards them. This will attract people towards you like a magnet.

Some people feel as if their life has no purpose. This feeling creates a distressing and depressing sense of emptiness and fear. But when you connect with your soul, you will uncover the purpose for your being that will remove all fear and feeling of emptiness. Having a purposeful life is the path to happiness.

Being connected with your soul will bring you into contact with the rich source of genius, talent and abilities that you have. Connecting with your soul will give you the confidence to mine this mother lode and develop your unique genius and talent to its fullest potential. When you begin to encounter your soul, you'll be be stirred to open up these talents and express them in the most gratifying and effective ways.

Connecting with your soul will make you a happier person because you'll acquire the wisdom to heal painful and negative feelings. You'll be able to deal with your emotions in an inspired and loving way and say "Yes!" to life.

How do you connect with your soul

Connecting with your soul is immensely fulfilling and rewarding and really not that difficult. Every morning, before getting up, spend time being aware of your deepest desires. Allow them to develop and flourish in your awareness and let them lead you in planning your day. As you get on with your day, search for the fulfillment of those desires and pursue them. As you pursue your desires, your soul will open the lines of communication and give you guidance.

Meditation – You can learn to connect with your soul if you learn to quiet yourself and step back a bit from the world around you. Switch off the radio and TV, don't access your Twitter or Facebook or any social network accounts, don't even open the newspaper. Put off reading your favorite book. Go to a quiet corner and give yourself a little quiet time alone and be still. From the stillness and quiet will arise answers to many issues and matters that plague your mind. Learn to meditate and cast the worldly matters out of your thoughts and be alone with yourself. Do this early in the morning, when everybody else at home is asleep and there is no one to disturb you.

Nourish your soul. Just like your body, your soul too needs sustenance. Read inspirational books that will nurture your soul. Watch the sunrise or sunset and appreciate the wonders of creation. Create beauty around you, perhaps as a vase full of fresh flowers in your work area. The act of choosing, picking and arranging flowers from your garden is, in itself meditation, nourishment of the soul. Write down a gratitude list every night before going to sleep. Remind yourself of all the blessings, big and small, that you've received.

Establish connection with others. Connect with people on a deeper level. Be more sympathetic and compassionate. Find people who are already in the advanced stages of connecting with their souls and learn from them. If you need to be connected with your soul, your soul also needs connection with others.

The more you give attention, time, and energy to connecting with your soul, the clearer and stronger will be your awareness of your deepest yearnings. You will also learn how to distinguish between soul and ego desires. Ego desires often result in momentary gratification while soul yearnings lead to enduring happiness and satisfaction. When you are in touch with your soul's desires your soul will reciprocate by opening more communication lines with you.

Conclusion

Genuine happiness can be achieved

So, do you have what it takes to be happy, really happy? I can assure you, genuine happiness can be achieved. It is already there within you. All you need to do is to discover it and live out these 7 secrets to happiness through practice:

1st – Live in the here and now - seize the moment

2nd – Be more assertive and tak charge of your life

3rd – Act as if everything you want in life is already present

4th – Don't take things personally

5th – Look at the bright side of life

6th – Love and take care of yourself

7th – Connect with your Inner Power or soul

You need to make a decision to choose happiness. No one else can do it for you. Fame, material wealth, accolade and praise from others can never give you genuine

happiness. You need to seek inner joy, peace, contentment, and fulfillment. Happiness is animated by the inner
workings of your mind and spirit. Nothing and nobody
else can hand it to you. You have to work at it so that it
becomes a reality for you.

So, Don't worry, Be happy!!!!!

www.ingramcontent.com/pod-product-compliance
Lightning Source LLC
Chambersburg PA
CBHW061151040426
42445CB00013B/1653